Collins
INTERNATIONAL
PRIMARY

Computing
Student's Book

1

Rebecca Franks, Dr Tracy Gardner and Liz Smart

William Collins' dream of knowledge for all began with the publication of his first book in 1819.

A self-educated mill worker, he not only enriched millions of lives, but also founded a flourishing publishing house. Today, staying true to this spirit, Collins books are packed with inspiration, innovation and practical expertise.

They place you at the centre of a world of possibility and give you exactly what you need to explore it.

Collins. Freedom to teach.

Published by Collins

An imprint of HarperCollins*Publishers*
The News Building, 1 London Bridge Street, London,
SE1 9GF, UK

HarperCollins*Publishers*
Macken House, 39/40 Mayor Street Upper, Dublin 1,
D01 C9W8, Ireland

This book contains FSC™ certified paper and other controlled sources to ensure responsible forest management.

For more information visit: harpercollins.co.uk/green

> Browse the complete Collins catalogue at
> **collins.co.uk**

© HarperCollins*Publishers* Limited 2024

10 9 8 7 6 5 4 3 2 1

ISBN 978-0-00-868384-9

All rights reserved. No part of this publication may be reproduced, stored in a retrieval system, or transmitted in any form by any means, electronic, mechanical, photocopying, recording or otherwise, without the prior written permission of the Publisher or a licence permitting restricted copying in the United Kingdom issued by the Copyright Licensing Agency Ltd, 5th Floor, Shackleton House, 4 Battle Bridge Lane, London SE1 2HX.

British Library Cataloguing-in-Publication Data

A catalogue record for this publication is available from the British Library.

Authors: Rebecca Franks, Dr Tracy Gardner and Liz Smart
Publisher: Catherine Martin
Product developer: Saaleh Patel
Development editor: Gemma Coleman
Project manager: Just Content Ltd
Copy editor: Tanya Solomons
Proofreader: Laura Connell
Cover designer: Gordon McGilp
Cover image: Amparo Barrera, Kneath Associates
Internal designer: Steve Evans, Planet Life Art
Illustration: Jouve India Ltd
Typesetter: Ken Vail Graphic Design
Production controller: Lyndsey Rogers
Printed and bound by Martins the Printers

Contents

Introduction: How to use this book

In the Collins Stage 1 Computing Student's Book and Workbook you will find lots of fun and interesting activities and projects, which will help you develop your Computing skills.

You will learn about these six key computing themes:

- Our digital world – learning about the tools we need to find our way around the digital world safely
- Content creation – finding out how to use different types of software
- Create with code – creating simple programs
- How computers work – understanding what goes on inside the computing devices we use
- Connect the world – discovering how the world is connected through networks, the internet and the World Wide Web
- The power of data – collecting, sorting and organising information to answer questions.

In each chapter, you will learn and practise new skills and create a final project. At the end of the chapter, you will share your project work with the class in a showcase. This will give you the chance to practise your presenting skills and get feedback on your work.

There are seven chapters in Stage 1 and these cover all six key computing themes – there are two chapters on creating with code.

In Stage 1 you will design a robot to help someone who works at your school, and plan a journey for a robot to take to tell a story. You will design and build an app that feeds a character their favourite foods and make an app to help with counting. You will write a computer program to show a view from a window in layers and design a webpage. You will work together as a class to collect, sort and organise information to plan a class celebration.

Key features of the Student's Book

On the first page of each chapter, you can read about what you are going to learn in the chapter and see examples of the final project.

Each lesson begins with a reminder of anything you have already learned about the topic.

Questions to talk about and a chance to share your ideas with your classmates.

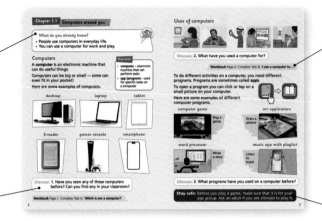

These are the Workbook tasks that you need to complete.

'Stay safe' tips remind you of possible dangers in the digital world.

At the end of each chapter, you will showcase your work, which means presenting your project to an audience.

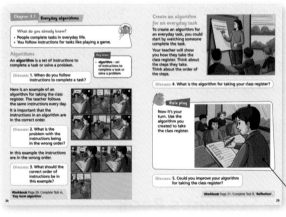

A time to think about what you have been learning and how you feel about your how you are getting on.

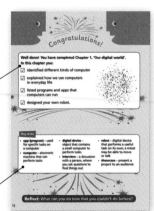

An activity where you act out real-world situations.

When you have completed a chapter, you can celebrate what you have achieved and look back at everything new that you have learned.

All the key terms from the chapter are listed together here to help you remember them.

Chapter 1

Our digital world

◐ Project: Design a robot to help someone who works at your school

In this chapter, you will:

- identify different kinds of computer
- explain how people use computers in everyday life
- list programs and apps that computers can run
- design your own robot.

End of chapter project:

Design a robot to help someone who works at your school

You will design something like these robots:

むかしむかし

What do you already know?

- People use computers in everyday life.
- You can use a computer for work and play.

Computers

A **computer** is an electronic machine that can do useful things.

Computers can be big or small — some can even fit in your pocket!

Here are some examples of computers.

Key terms

- **computer** – electronic machine that can perform tasks
- **app (program)** – used for specific tasks on a computer

desktop

laptop

tablet

E-reader

games console

smartphone

Discuss: 1. Have you seen any of these computers before? Can you find any in your classroom?

Workbook Page 1: Complete Task A, '**Which is not a computer?**'.

Uses of computers

Discuss: 2. What have you used a computer for?

Workbook Page 2: Complete Task B, '**I use a computer to…**'.

To do different activities on a computer, you need different programs. Programs are sometimes called **apps**.

To open a program you can click or tap on a small picture on your computer.

Here are some examples of different computer programs.

computer game

Play a game

art application

Draw a picture

word processor

Write a story

music app with playlist

Listen to music

Discuss: 3. What programs have you used on a computer before?

Stay safe: Before you play a game, make sure that it is for your age group. Ask an adult if you are allowed to play it.

> **What do you already know?**
>
> - Laptops, tablets and smartphones are computers.
> - Computers come in different shapes and sizes.
> - You can use computers for lots of different things, such as playing games and listening to music.

Digital devices around you

There are **digital devices** all around you. Digital devices are objects that contain small computers to control what they do.

Here are some examples of digital devices.

Key terms

- **digital device** – object that contains a small computer to perform tasks
- **robot** – digital device that performs a useful task on its own; it may be able to move or talk

air conditioning

Makes the air cooler on hot days

washing machine

Uses water and soap to make dirty clothes clean

supermarket checkout

Works out the total cost of scanned shopping items

CCTV

Cameras watch to see if anything bad is happening

satellite navigation

A digital map that helps you find the way to places

> **Discuss:** 4. Which of these digital devices have you seen? Can you think of any more digital devices?

Robots

Robots are a type of digital device. They can do different tasks on their own! A computer first needs to tell the robot what to do and how to do it.

Here are some examples of robots.

mail-sorting robot

food-delivery robot

ocean-cleaning robot

> **Discuss:** 5. Have you seen a robot in the real world?
> Can you think of any more real-life robots?

> **Discuss:** 6. Can you find all the robots in the pictures?
> There are three robots in each picture.

Workbook Pages 3 and 4: Complete Task A, **'Digital devices and robots around you'**.

What do you already know?

- A robot is a digital device that performs a useful task on its own.
- A robot may be able to move or talk.
- Robots can help humans with tasks.

Designing a robot

Key terms

- **interview** – a discussion with a person, where you ask questions to find things out

End of chapter project:

Design a robot to help someone who works at your school.

Your project is to design a robot to help someone with an everyday task. You will ask a person questions to find out how to help them. Asking questions for a purpose is called an **interview**.

Here is an example of an interview.

Discuss: 7. How do school meals work in our school?

Plan the interview

You will interview a person about their job. Your questions will help you understand their job.

Discuss: 8. What questions could you ask the person about the job they do every day at school?

Your teacher will write down your ideas for your class interview.

The interview

Now it is time for the interview! Your teacher will introduce a guest. You will take turns asking the questions from your class list of questions.

Workbook Pages 5 and 6: Complete Task A, '**The interview**'.

Discuss: 9. What did you learn from the interview with your guest? Were there any surprises?

Reflect: What have you learned about asking questions and listening to other people?

> **What do you already know?**
>
> - A robot is a digital device that performs a useful task on its own.
> - A robot may be able to move or talk.
> - Robots can help humans with tasks.

What can a robot do?

Robots can help with many tasks. Some robots can move. Some robots can listen and talk. Here are some examples of what robots can do.

Discuss: 10. What everyday tasks would a robot be good at? Are there any tasks you do every day that a robot could do?

What tasks does your guest do?

Workbook Pages 5 and 6: Look at your completed Task A, '**The Interview**', from Chapter 1.3.

Discuss: 11. What did you learn about the tasks your guest does?

Discuss: 12. How could a robot help your guest?

Choose a task

Workbook Pages 7 and 8: Complete Task A, '**Choose a task to help your guest with**'.

Discuss: 13. Why did you choose your task? How will the robot help your guest?

End of chapter project:

Design a robot to help someone who works at your school.

Remember, you will design something like these robots.

Discuss: 14. What task did you decide your robot should carry out to help your guest?

Workbook Page 9: Complete Task A, '**Sketch your robot ideas**'.

Workbook Page 10: Complete Task B, '**Draw your final design**'.

What does it mean to showcase your project?

Showcasing means sharing your project with other people.

Tips for showcasing your project:

- Be prepared to answer questions about your project.
- Hold your workbook up to show your design. Pictures are a great way to share designs.
- Try your best to talk clearly and loudly enough for everyone to hear.

Showcase: You should:
- talk about your robot design
- say how your robot will help your guest with an everyday task.

Workbook Page 11: Complete Task A, '**Reflection**'.

Congratulations!

Well done! You have completed Chapter 1, 'Our digital world'.
In this chapter you:

☑ identified different kinds of computer

☑ explained how we use computers in everyday life

☑ listed programs and apps that computers can run

☑ designed your own robot.

Key terms

- **app (program)** – used for specific tasks on a computer

- **computer** – electronic machine that can perform tasks

- **digital device** – object that contains a small computer to perform tasks

- **interview** – a discussion with a person, where you ask questions to find things out

- **robot** – digital device that performs a useful task on its own; a robot may be able to move or talk

- **showcase** – present a project to an audience

Reflect: What can you do now that you couldn't do before?

Chapter 2
Content creation

○ Project: Design and build an app that feeds a character their favourite foods

In this chapter, you will:

- use a password to log on and off a computer
- save and open documents
- choose pictures for an app
- use a keyboard to type
- use a mouse to drag and drop.

End of chapter project:

Design and build an app that feeds a character their favourite foods

You will choose food items for an app that feeds a character their favourite food. Here are some examples of what you might create:

Feed Frank Strawberry, Melon, and Taco

Feed Frank Orange, Muffin, and Banana

Feed Frank Banana, Jam, and Honey

> **What do you already know?**
>
> • A computer is an electronic machine that you can use to perform tasks.

What is a password?

Computers contain lots of information that might be personal to you. You can use a **password** to keep your personal information safe. A password is a secret word you can use to keep your information safe.

Key terms

- **password** – secret code you use to keep your information safe
- **log on** – entering a username and password to use a computer
- **username** – personal name you use to access your information, for example to use a computer at school
- **log off** – exiting a computer when you have finished using it

Discuss: 1. Have you used a password before? Have you seen an adult use a password?

Discuss: 2. Do you use any passwords at school?

A good password

A good password should be easy for you to remember but hard for someone else to guess.

One way to make a password easy to remember is to use three random words.

For example:

FlowerSkyTrain

Workbook Page 12: Complete Task A, '**Three random pictures**'.

Switch on, log on and log off

After switching on your computer, you will need to **log on** by entering a **username** and a password.

For example:

When you log on with your username you will be able to see your information.

When you have finished using your computer you should always **log off**. When you log off, nobody else can see your information.

Your teacher will now show you how to log on and log off on the computers at your school.

Workbook Page 13: Complete Task B, '**Key terms practice**'.

Discuss: 3. What makes a good password?

Stay safe: Always keep your password a secret.

What do you already know?

- An app (program) does a specific task on a computer.

End of chapter project:

Design and build an app that feeds a character their favourite foods.

We have created the code for an app called 'Feed Frank'. Your job is to choose the foods that the app will use.

Here are the foods that you can choose from.

Key terms

- **capital letters** – big letters that we use at the start of a sentence or a name. Capital letters are bigger than lowercase letters.
- **lowercase letters** – smaller letters that we use most of the time when we write and type. Lowercase letters are smaller than capital letters.

Discuss: 4. Which three food items do you think you will pick?

Workbook Page 14: Complete Task A, '**Choose three foods**'.

Capital letters and lowercase letters

When you write with your hand or type on a keyboard you can use two types of letter. You can use **capital letters** or a **lowercase letters**.

Capital letters are bigger than lowercase letters. We use capital letters at the start of a sentence or name.

Lowercase letters are smaller than capital letters. We use lowercase letters most of the time when we write or type.

Below is a capital T and a lowercase t.

T	t

Discuss: 5. What is different about these two letters?

Write your food words

Your app will ask you to type the name of your chosen foods. Practise writing your chosen foods in your workbook.

Workbook Page 15: Complete Task B, '**Write your food words**'.

What do you already know?

- Capital letters are bigger than lowercase letters. We use capital letters at the start of a sentence or name.
- Lowercase letters are smaller than capital letters. We use lowercase letters most of the time when we write or type.

Using a word processor

A **word processor** is a program we use to type words into a computer. When you type words into a word processor, you can use capital letters and lowercase letters.

A keyboard has a button called 'caps lock'.

Key terms

- **word processor** – a program you use to type words into a computer to create a document

The 'caps lock' key is used to switch between capital letters and lowercase letters.

Discuss: 6. Has anyone used a word processor before? If so, what did you use it for?

Your teacher will show you how to type capital and lowercase letters using your school computers.

Type your food words

Your project is to 'Design and build an app that feeds a character their favourite foods'. Last lesson, you chose three foods to feed your character. You picked three from these options:

Taco

Melon

Muffin

Strawberry **Honey** **Orange** **Jam**

Donut **Apple** **Banana**

Your teacher will show you how to type your food words into the word processor using the keyboard.

Workbook Page 16: Complete Task A, '**Find the capital letters**'.

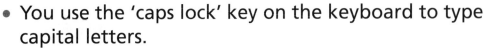

What do you already know?

- You use the 'caps lock' key on the keyboard to type capital letters.
- A computer has many programs that help you do different things. For example, a word processor program helps you to type lots of words.

Scratch

To build your app, you will use a program called **Scratch**. Scratch is a program that helps you to make fun projects.

You can use Scratch on a tablet computer or a desktop computer.

> **Discuss:** 7. Have you used Scratch before? If not, are you excited to use Scratch?

Key terms

- **Scratch** – program that allows you to create your own programs or apps
- **open** – view a file on a computer
- **save** – save a file on a computer so that you can use it again next time
- **sprite** – character or object in Scratch
- **stage** – area in Scratch where you can play with your app
- **costume** – different options for how your sprite looks in Scratch. It is like the clothes you wear each day!

Opening projects

In Scratch you can **open** projects that you or someone else have already created. You can then make changes to them. You will make changes to a Scratch project called 'Feed Frank'.

Your teacher will show you how to open the 'Feed Frank' project.

Saving projects

In Scratch you can **save** a project that you are working on. This means that you can open it again to use in the future.

You should save your work often in case something happens to your computer.

Your teacher will show you how to save your work.

The Scratch layout

Scratch has three main areas: Editor, **Sprites** and **Stage**.

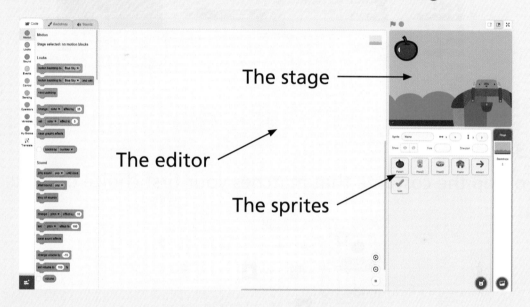

The stage

The editor

The sprites

Sprites

A sprite is a **character** or object in Scratch.

Look closely at the 'Sprites' area. Can you see three food sprites and Frank?

Each sprite has many costumes to choose from. A costume allows you to choose different pictures for your sprite.

Choose your costumes

Step 1

Click or tap on the 'Food1' sprite.

Step 2

Click or tap on the 'Costumes' tab.

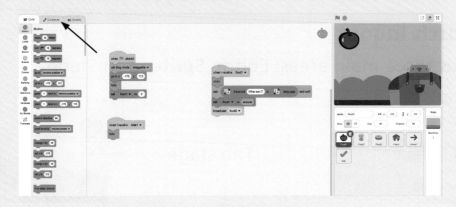

Step 3

Click or tap the costume that matches your first choice of food.

Step 4

In our example, we have chosen the 'Donut' as our first food choice. You can see that the 'Donut' now appears on the 'Food1' sprite.

Your 'Food1' sprite should show the costume that you chose.

Step 5

Choose a food costume for the 'Food2' and 'Food3' sprites.

Step 6

Save your work.

Workbook Page 17: Complete Task A, **'Scratch quiz'**.

What do you already know?

- Scratch is a program that you can use to create your own programs or apps.
- Scratch has sprites that can have many different costumes.
- You can choose a costume for a sprite by clicking on the sprite and then going to the 'Costumes' tab.
- To enter a capital letter on a keyboard, you use the 'caps lock'.

Play 'Feed Frank'

Your teacher will show you how to open your Scratch project from last lesson.

To play with your app, you need to click on the green flag at the top of the stage.

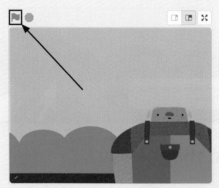

1. The program will run. A food item will appear. The food item will ask you 'What am I?'. A box will appear at the bottom for you to type the name of your food.

2. Type the name of the food into the box. Press 'Enter' on the keyboard.

3. Do the same for the other two foods.

Click and hold or tap and hold. Then drag the food items to feed frank.

Frank will like the food that he eats!

Workbook Page 18: Complete Task A, '**Rate your progress**'.

What do you already know?

- Showcasing is a way of sharing your project with other people.

Showcase your project

Remember, showcasing means sharing your project with other people.

Showcase: Showcase your 'Feed Frank' app, You should:
- say why you chose the three foods for your app
- let the player use the app and have fun.

Workbook Page 19: Complete Task A, '**Reflection**'.

Congratulations!

**Well done! You have completed Chapter 2, 'Content creation'.
In this chapter you:**

☑ used a password to log on and log off on a computer

☑ made design choices for an app

☑ saved and opened documents

☑ used a keyboard to type

☑ used a mouse to drag and drop.

Key terms

- **capital letters** – big letters that we use at the start of a sentence or a name. Capital letters are bigger than lowercase letters.
- **costume** – different options for how your sprite looks in Scratch. It is like the clothes you wear each day!
- **log off** – exiting a computer when you have finished using it
- **log on** – entering a username and password to use a computer
- **lowercase letters** – smaller letters that we use most of the time when we write and type. Lowercase letters are smaller than capital letters.
- **open** – view a file on a computer

- **password** – secret code you use to keep your information safe
- **save** – save a file on a computer so that you can use it again next time
- **Scratch** – program that allows you to create your own programs or apps
- **sprite** – character or object in Scratch
- **stage** – area in Scratch where you can play with your app
- **username** – personal name you use to access your information, for example to use a computer at school
- **word processor** – a program you use to type words into a computer to create a document

Reflect: How did it feel to showcase your app to other learners in the class?

Chapter 3

Create with code 1

Project: Plan a journey for a Bee-Bot to take to tell a story

In this chapter, you will:

- role-play an algorithm for an everyday task
- recreate an algorithm as code on a robot
- predict paths that a Bee-Bot will take
- create a journey for a Bee-Bot that follows a story.

End of chapter project:

Plan a journey for a Bee-Bot to take to tell a story

Your story area will look something like these examples:

What do you already know?

- People complete tasks in everyday life.
- You follow instructions for tasks like playing a game.

Algorithms

An **algorithm** is a set of instructions to complete a task or solve a problem.

Key terms

- **algorithm** – set of instructions to complete a task or solve a problem

Discuss: 1. When do you follow instructions to complete a task?

Here is an example of an algorithm for taking the class register. The teacher follows the same instructions every day.

It is important that the instructions in an algorithm are in the correct order.

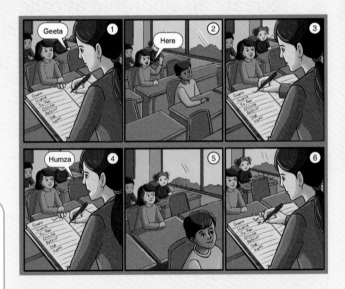

Discuss: 2. What is the problem with the instructions being in the wrong order?

In this example the instructions are in the wrong order.

Discuss: 3. What should the correct order of instructions be in this example?

Workbook Page 20: Complete Task A, '**Key term algorithm**'.

Create an algorithm for an everyday task

To create an algorithm for an everyday task, you could start by watching someone complete the task.

Your teacher will show you how they take the class register. Think about the steps they take. Think about the order of the steps.

Discuss: 4. What is the algorithm for taking your class register?

Role play

Now it's your turn. Use the algorithm you created to take the class register.

Discuss: 5. Could you improve your algorithm for taking the class register?

Workbook Page 21: Complete Task B, '**Reflection**'.

What do you already know?

- A computer is an electronic machine that can perform tasks.
- A robot is a digital device that performs a useful task on its own. A robot may be able to move or talk.
- An algorithm is a set of instructions to complete a task or solve a problem.
- The order of instructions in an algorithm is important.

What is code?

Computers and robots use **code** to know how to complete a task or solve a problem.

You need to enter the code in a way that the computer or robot understands.

Introducing the Bee-Bot

A **Bee-Bot** is a robot that uses code to move.

You can enter code into the Bee-Bot by pressing buttons. The buttons have direction arrows on them.

Key terms

- **code** – instructions that tell a computer what to do
- **Bee-Bot** – robot that uses code to move in different directions

Discuss: 6. Have you seen a robot like the Bee-Bot before? What was it doing?

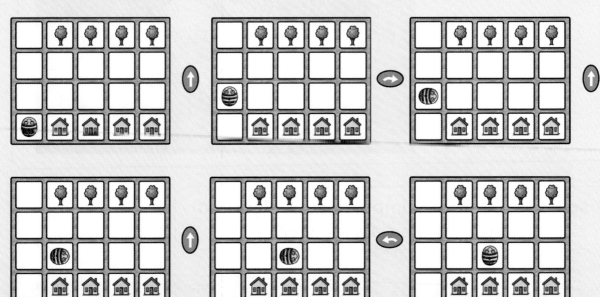

Bee-Bot buttons

Your teacher will show you a Bee-Bot. They will enter code into the Bee-Bot by pressing buttons. When the code runs the Bee-Bot will move.

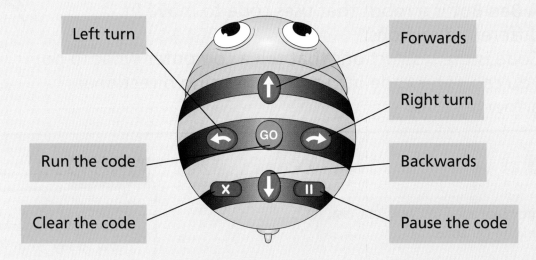

Left turn

Forwards

Right turn

Run the code

Backwards

Clear the code

Pause the code

Workbook Page 22: Complete Task A, '**Follow a path**'.

Enter code into a Bee-Bot

Enter the code below into your Bee-Bot so that it follows the path.

Clear the code. Now try this code.

Clear the code. Now try this code.

Discuss: 7. What would happen if you didn't clear the code?

Workbook Page 23: Complete Task B, '**Create a path**'.

Discuss: 8. Did you make any mistakes entering the code? What do you need to do if you make a mistake?

What do you already know?

- A Bee-Bot is a robot that uses code to move in different directions.
- Code is the instructions that tell a computer what to do.
- You can enter code into a Bee-Bot using directional arrow buttons.

Predict the code

Workbook Page 24: Complete Task A, '**Label the buttons**'.

A Bee-Bot moves forward 15 cm for each press of the 'Forwards' arrow button. This information is useful to **predict** the code you need.

Key terms

- **predict** – use information you have now to say what is going to happen in the future

You can use this information to predict how many times you need to press the forwards button for the Bee-Bot to reach an object.

Your teacher will place an object on the floor in front of your Bee-Bot.

Workbook Page 24: Complete Task B, '**Predict the code: forwards**'.

Discuss: 9. How did you predict the number of button presses? Did you use the information that the Bee-Bot moves 15 cm each step?

Predict more code

Use your prediction skills to predict the code the Bee-Bot needs to reach another object.

This time the Bee-Bot needs you to enter code using more than one arrow button.

The left and right arrow buttons turn the Bee-Bot left and right. They do not move the Bee-Bot left and right.

Each left or right arrow button press turns the Bee-Bot one quarter turn.

Your teacher will place an object on the floor for your Bee-Bot to move towards.

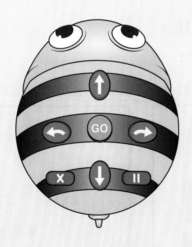

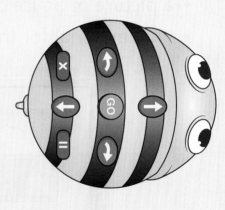

Workbook Page 25: Complete Task C, '**Predict the code: more than one direction**'.

Discuss: 10. How did you create a prediction for how many moves the Bee-Bot needs to make to move to an object?

Workbook Page 25: Complete Task D, '**Reflect**'.

What do you already know?

- A Bee-Bot is a robot that uses code to move in different directions.
- You can use code to turn and move a Bee-Bot.

End of chapter project:

Plan a journey for a Bee-Bot to take to tell a story.

Your project is to create a story using objects. You will enter code into your Bee-Bot to tell the story. You will use three objects.

This example story uses:

- a picture of a crab

- a picture of an ice cream

- blue material for the sea.

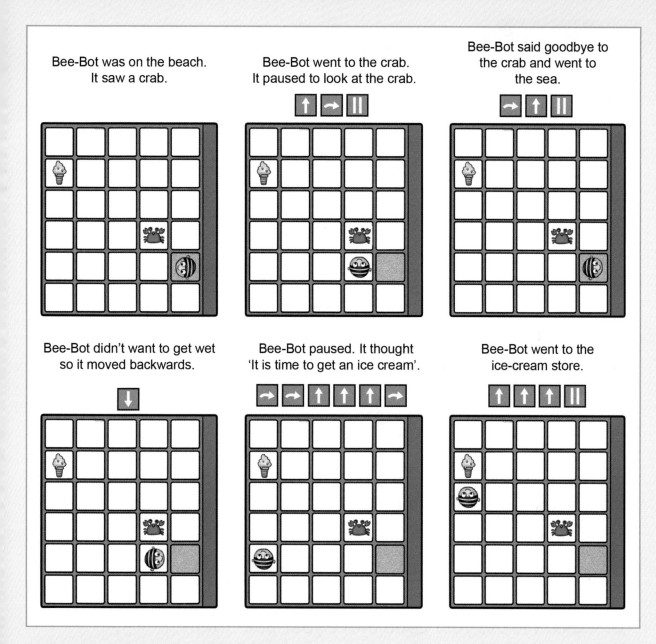

Bee-Bot was on the beach. It saw a crab.

Bee-Bot went to the crab. It paused to look at the crab.

Bee-Bot said goodbye to the crab and went to the sea.

Bee-Bot didn't want to get wet so it moved backwards.

Bee-Bot paused. It thought 'It is time to get an ice cream'.

Bee-Bot went to the ice-cream store.

Each time you press the 'Pause the code' button it stops the Bee-Bot for one second.

Workbook Page 26: Complete Task A, '**Plan your story**'.

Stay safe: You could make a story about staying safe online. The Bee-Bot could first get a username, then a password, and then it could open an app.

What do you already know?

• We use code to turn and move a Bee-Bot.

Plan your journey

Now it is time to plan your Bee-Bot's journey. Here are some examples:

Place your starting marker and the three objects on the floor. You can use a piece of paper to mark the starting position for your Bee-Bot.

Workbook Page 27: Complete task A, '**Code for your first object**'.

Discuss: 11. Did your code move your Bee-Bot in the way you wanted it to move? Do you have any tips to share with the class?

Workbook Page 28: Complete task B, '**Code for your second object**'.

Workbook Page 29: Complete task C, '**Code for your third object**'.

Discuss: 12. What problems did you have with your code? How did you fix them?

> **What do you already know?**
>
> - Showcasing is a way of sharing your project with other people.

Showcase your project

Remember, showcasing means sharing your project with other people.

You are going to be a storyteller. You will tell your story of the Bee-Bot's journey to the class.

Tips for storytelling:

- If you are working in a group, have more than one storyteller – you could each say one line.
- Use props – show your objects as you tell your story.

> **Showcase:** You should:
> - tell your story
> - talk about the code you created
> - give an example of a problem that you fixed.

Workbook Page 30: Complete Task A, '**Reflection**'.

Congratulations!

Well done! You have completed Chapter 3, 'Create with code 1'.

In this chapter you:

- ☑ role-played an algorithm for an everyday task

- ☑ recreated an algorithm as code on a robot

- ☑ predicted paths that a Bee-Bot will take

- ☑ created a journey for a Bee-Bot that follows a story.

Key terms

- **algorithm** – set of instructions to complete a task or solve a problem

- **Bee-Bot** – robot that uses code to move in different directions
- **code** – instructions that tell a computer what to do

- **predict** – use information you have now to say what is going to happen in the future

Reflect: What do you need to remember the next time you write code for a Bee-Bot?

Chapter 4

How computers work

○ Project: Make a counting app to help with counting from 1 to 5

In this chapter, you will:

- identify different components of a computer system
- describe computer inputs and outputs
- record sounds and select costumes for sprites
- make your own counting app.

End of chapter project:

Make a counting app to help with counting from 1 to 5

You will make a counting app. It will use recordings of your voice and character costumes that you have chosen. Here are some examples of what you might create:

1

3

4

What do you already know?

- A computer is an electronic machine that can perform tasks.

Computer systems

A **computer system** is a computer with its different parts. The parts of a computing system are called **components**.

computer

mouse

keyboard

screen (or monitor)

printer

speakers

touchpad (or trackpad)

touchscreen

Key terms

- **computer system** – computer with its connected parts
- **component** – part of a computer system
- **mouse** – component that you move to point to things on a computer screen
- **keyboard** – component that you use to type letters and numbers on a computer
- **screen (or monitor)** – component that shows pictures and videos from a computer
- **printer** – component that can put pictures and words on paper
- **speakers** – component that can play sound from a computer
- **touchpad (or trackpad)** – part of a laptop computer that you use to point to things on a computer screen by moving your finger

headphones

webcam

microphone

Key terms

- **touchscreen** – component that shows pictures and videos and allows you to point to things with your finger
- **headphones** – component that can play sound from a computer
- **microphone** – component that can get sound into a computer
- **webcam** – component that can get pictures and video into a computer
- **input** – component that allows a person to enter information into a computer
- **output** – component that presents information to a person

Discuss: 1. Which of these components have you seen or used before? Which one do you like using the most?

Inputs and outputs

An **input** is a component that allows a person to enter information into a computer.

An **output** is a component that provides information to a person.

A screen is an output because text, images and videos are presented on it. A keyboard is an input because it sends key presses into the computer.

Workbook Page 31: Complete Task A, '**Find the inputs**'.

Workbook Page 32: Complete Task B, '**Find the outputs**'.

Discuss: 2. How can you remember the difference between an input and an output?

What do you already know?

- Your computer can run apps.
- Scratch is a computer program that you can use to create apps.
- You use inputs to enter information into a computer.
- You use outputs to provide information from a computer.

Remember: Inputs and outputs

Discuss: 3. Can you name an input?

A mouse, touchpad and touchscreen are all inputs. You can click or tap them.

Discuss: 4. Can you name an output?

The screen and speakers are outputs on a computer or tablet.

Remember: Scratch

Scratch is a computer program that you can use to create your own apps.

In this lesson you will use an app that has been created for you.

Investigate a Scratch app

You are going to investigate a Scratch app that uses your computer's inputs and outputs.

Your teacher will tell you how to open the Scratch app.

Stay safe: Check with a grown-up before you use an app.

When you have opened the app it should look like this:

The Scratch app has six sprites that you can click or tap on.

Workbook Page 33: Complete Task A, '**Investigate a Scratch app**'.

Workbook Page 34: Complete Task B, '**Which of these inputs did you use?**' and Task C, '**Which of these outputs did you use?**'.

Discuss: 5. Which inputs and outputs did the Scratch app use?

> **What do you already know?**
> - A microphone is an input.
> - Speakers are an output.

Scratch can record sounds

Remember, Scratch is a computer program that you can use to create your own apps. In this lesson, you will use the Sound Editor in Scratch to record your voice.

> **Discuss:** 6. Is a microphone an input or an output? Why?

Your teacher will give you instructions to open the Scratch project.

Record a sound in Scratch

You will record your voice saying "Hello".

Click Sounds to open the Scratch Sound Editor.

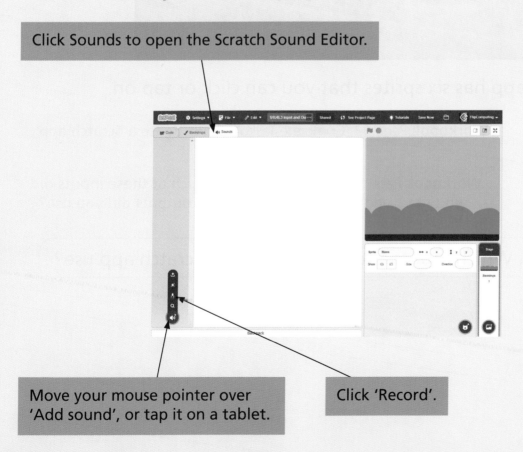

Move your mouse pointer over 'Add sound', or tap it on a tablet.

Click 'Record'.

1. If Scratch asks for permission to use your microphone, click 'Allow'.

2. Now you are going to record your voice. Get ready! Click Record, say "Hello" and then click "Stop recording".

 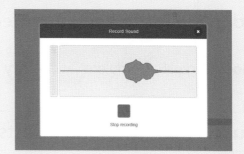

3. Click 'Play'. If you want to try again, click 'Re-record'.

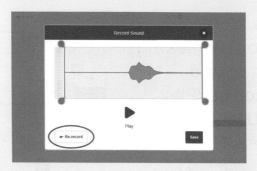

4. When you are happy with your sound recording, click 'Save'.

5. You can play your sound in the Sound Editor by clicking 'Play'.

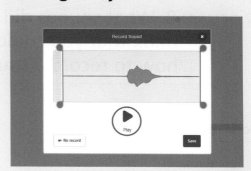

Add sound effects

You can add sound effects to a recorded sound.

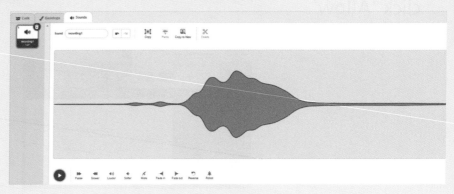

Click the 'Faster' and 'Slower' buttons until you get to your favourite speed.

Click the 'Louder' and 'Softer' buttons until the sound is loud enough but not too loud.

If you don't want to keep an effect, click 'Undo'.

Workbook Page 35: Complete Task A, '**Try sound effects**'.

Discuss: 7. Which sound effects did you like best?

Record more sounds

Record more sounds. You can choose what to say or try making a noise. Try different sound effects. Remember to use 'Play' to listen to sounds. Use 'Undo' if you don't like the result.

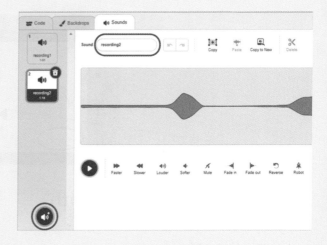

You can click on 'recording1' or 'recording2' to move between your sound recordings.

Discuss: 8. What sounds did you record? Do you think that you could show someone else how to record a sound in Scratch now?

Workbook Page 36: Complete Task B, '**Match the pictures**'.

What do you already know?

- We call characters or objects in Scratch sprites.
- Sprites appear on the Stage.
- A costume is a picture for a sprite.

End of chapter project:

Make a counting app to help with counting from 1 to 5.

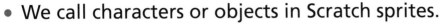

Discuss: 9. Which inputs and outputs on your computer will the project use?

Choose costumes

You will now choose the costumes for your sprites.

Workbook Page 37: Complete Task A, '**Choose costumes for your app**'.

Your teacher will tell you how to open the Scratch project for this lesson.

1. Click on Sprite 1.

2. Click 'Costumes'.

3. Find the costume you chose in the Workbook and click on it.

Notice that Sprite 1 has changed to use the new costume.

Change the costumes for the other sprites to match the sprites you chose in the Workbook.

Save your project.

Discuss: 10. Why did you choose the costumes that you did? Were you able to find the costumes that you needed?

> **What do you already know?**
> - You can record sounds in Scratch.
> - You can add sound effects to sounds in Scratch.

Record sounds

Last lesson you chose costumes for your sprites and saved your app. You will now record sounds so that your sprites can say the numbers from 1 to 5.

Your teacher will show you how to open your Scratch counting app.

1. Click on Sprite 1.

2. Click on Sounds.

3. Record yourself saying the word "one".

4. If you would like to add an effect then you can do this now.

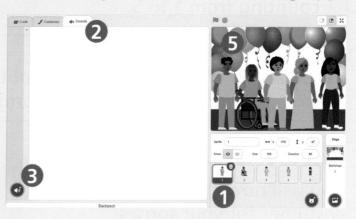

5. Click on Sprite 1 on the Stage to play the sound.

6. Repeat the same steps for Sprites 2, 3, 4 and 5. Make sure you record the correct number for the correct sprite!

Save your project.

Workbook Page 38: Complete Task A, '**Record sounds one to five**'.

Workbook Page 39: Complete Task B, '**Where should you click?**'.

> **Discuss:** 11. Is it important for a counting app to use children's voices? Why do you think that?

What do you already know?

- An input is a component that allows a person to enter information into a computer.
- An output is a component that provides information to a person.
- You can create a counting app in Scratch.
- Showcasing is a way of sharing your project with other people.

Showcase your project

Remember, showcasing means sharing your project with other people.

Tips for showcasing your project:

- Explain which sprite you are clicking or tapping on.
- Do your best to talk clearly and loudly enough for everyone to hear.
- Listen carefully when watching someone else's showcase and celebrate their ideas.

Showcase: Showcase your counting app. You should:
- click on two or more sprites to show that they say the correct number
- explain why you chose one of the sprite costumes.

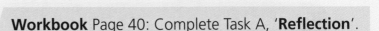

Workbook Page 40: Complete Task A, '**Reflection**'.

Congratulations!

Well done! You have completed Chapter 4, 'How computers work'. In this chapter you:

☑ identified different components of a computing system

☑ described computer inputs and outputs

☑ recorded sounds and selected costumes for sprites

☑ made your own counting app.

Key terms

- **component** – part of a computer system
- **computer system** – computer with its connected parts
- **headphones** – component that can play sound from a computer
- **input** – component that allows a person to enter information into a computer
- **keyboard** – component that you use to type letters and numbers on a computer

- **microphone** – component that can get sound into a computer
- **mouse** – component that you move to point to things on a computer screen
- **output** – component that presents information to a person
- **printer** – component that can put pictures and words on paper
- **screen (or monitor)** – component that shows pictures and videos from a computer

- **speakers** – component that can play sound from a computer
- **touchpad (or trackpad)** – part of a laptop computer that you use to point to things on a computer screen by moving your finger
- **touchscreen** – component that shows pictures and videos and allows you to point to things with your finger
- **webcam** – component that can get pictures and video into a computer

Reflect: How does it feel to have made your own app?

Chapter 5

Create with code 2

● Project: Create a scene with layers to show a view from a window

In this chapter, you will:

- describe why the order of instructions is important
- identify errors in code and fix them
- design and build an app that creates a scene from a window.

End of chapter project:

Create a scene with layers to show a view from a window

You will design something like these window scenes:

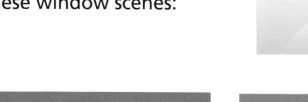

What do you already know?

- An algorithm is a set of instructions to complete a task or solve a problem.
- Programs use instructions that are called 'code'.
- Scratch is a program that allows you to create your own programs or apps.

Order is important

Remember, you must write instructions, or algorithms, in the correct order.

Key terms

- **code block** – single line of code in Scratch

Discuss: 1. What is the correct order for putting on your shoes and socks?

Stacking rings

Order is important for this stacking rings toy. The rings are only in the correct order if you place the rings on the toy with the largest ring at the bottom and the smallest ring at the top.

Your teacher will ask you to provide instructions for completing the stacking toy game.

Workbook Page 41: Complete Task A, '**Stack the rings**'.

Stacking tower in Scratch

A stacking tower toy has been created in Scratch. **Code blocks** have been created to place the rings in order. When you click the green flag ⚑, the rings are stacked in the wrong order.

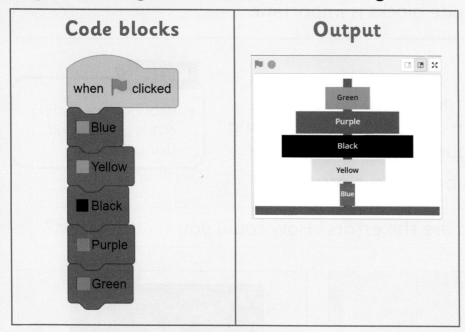

Code blocks	Output

Discuss: 2. Can you spot what is wrong with the order of the stacking rings? Why do you think this is?

Try it yourself!

Your teacher will show you how to open the Scratch project.

You can click and drag or tap and drag code blocks to reorder them.

Workbook Page 42: Complete Task B, '**The correct order**'.

Reflect: How many times did you change the blocks before you found the correct order?

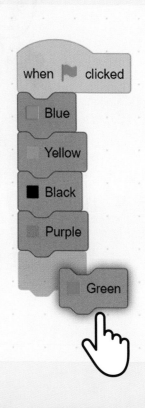

> **What do you already know?**
> - The order of code blocks is important.

Debugging

It is very common for code to have errors. We can fix errors in code. Finding and fixing errors is called **debugging**.

The three pictures below have errors.

Key terms

- **debugging** – finding errors in code and fixing them

> **Discuss:** 3. What are the errors? How could you fix the errors?

1+1=3

Debugging Scratch code

A child has made a sand bucket animation in Scratch. They want the bucket of sand to fill up from the bottom to the top.

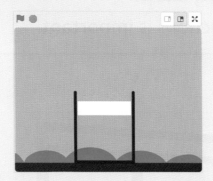

The order that the bucket should fill up is brown, orange, yellow then white.

The white layer of sand has appeared first. There is an error in the code.

Your teacher will show you how to open the Scratch project and run it yourself.

Workbook Page 43: Complete Task A, '**Find the error**'.

Workbook Page 44: Complete Task B, '**Fix the error**'.

Reflect: What error did you find? Why should you test your code again after you fix it?

What do you already know?

• The order of instructions is important.

Order is important

Key terms

• **layers** – placing objects on top of each other, for example a cake could have three layers of sponge

Discuss: 4. Look out of the window. What is the furthest thing away that you can see?

Discuss: 5. Which objects are closest to the window?

When you design your own scenes, the order is really important. Objects that are furthest away go at the back. Objects that are close go at the front.

This jungle scene has four **layers**. You have to place the layers in the correct order so that you can see the whole scene.

Layer 1
Layer 2
Layer 3
Layer 4

If you place the layers in the wrong order, the scene won't look right.

Layer 4
Layer 1
Layer 2
Layer 3

Layered scenes

You can use layers to create pieces of artwork like these examples:

> **Discuss:** 6. Have you seen artwork like this before? If so, can you describe it?

You are now going to make your own layered scene artwork.

Workbook Page 45: Complete Task A, '**Order the layers**'.

Your teacher will provide you with materials to create your own layered scene.

What do you already know?

- The order of instructions is important.
- You can use layers to create artwork.
- A Scratch program can have many sprites.
- Sprites can have many costumes.

End of chapter project:

Create a scene with layers to show a view from a window.

You will choose a window frame, an animal, a tree and a background for your layered scene.

Your teacher will show you the Scratch project to help you see what you are going to make.

Discuss: 7. What would happen if you placed the background last?

Workbook Pages 46 and 47: Complete Task A, '**Choose your costumes**'.

Workbook Page 47: Complete Task B, '**Order your sprites**'.

Reflect: Do you think that you have ordered your sprites correctly? Share your work with a partner and check your order.

What do you already know?

- Scratch is a program that allows you to create your own programs or apps.
- Scratch has sprites.
- Sprites have many costumes.
- The order that you place code blocks is important.

Choose your costumes

Your teacher will show you how to open the Scratch project, which you can use to choose your costumes.

Step 1

Find the four sprites that you will use for the layers of the scene.

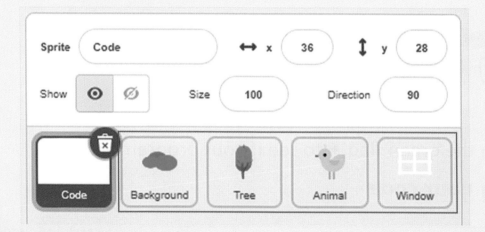

Step 2

For each sprite, select the costume that you chose last lesson in your Workbook. Remember, to select a costume, you click or tap on the Costumes tab.

Workbook Page 48: Complete Task A, '**Order the code blocks**'.

Order the code blocks in Scratch

Now you need to decide the correct order for the code blocks to display your window.

Workbook Page 49: Complete Task A, '**Order the code blocks**'.

Step 1

Click on the 'Code' sprite.

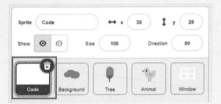

Step 2

Drag the code blocks in the Code area into the correct order.

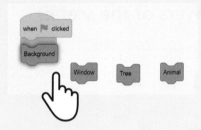

Step 3

Click on the green flag ⚑ to see if your program works.

Debug your code

> **Discuss:** 8. Did your program work? If not, do you know what went wrong?

Workbook Page 49: Complete Task B, '**Test your code**'.

Your teacher will show you how to save your work.

> **Reflect:** Did you get your order right the first time? If not, what did you need to change to make it work?

> **Stay safe:** Remember to always log off from your computer when you have finished using it.

> **What do you already know?**
> - Showcasing is a way of sharing your project with other people.

Showcase your project

Remember, showcasing means sharing your project with other people.

Tips for showcasing your project:

- Speak clearly and loudly enough for everyone to hear.
- Allow your user to click the green flag to see what happens.
- Practise what you will say for your showcase.

> **Showcase:** Showcase your scene app. You should:
> - say why you chose the costumes that you did
> - say how the project makes you feel – calm? warm? cool? happy?
> - talk about any errors you spotted and fixed.

Workbook Page 50: Complete Task A, '**Reflection**'.

Congratulations!

Well done! You have completed Chapter 5 'Create with code 2'.
In this chapter you:

- ☑ described why the order of instructions was important

- ☑ identified errors in code and fixed them

- ☑ designed and built an app that creates a scene from a window.

Key terms

- **code block** – single line of code in Scratch

- **debugging** – finding errors in code and fixing them

- **layers** – placing objects on top of each other, for example a cake could have three layers of sponge

Reflect: Which was your favourite part of making your app? Why?

Chapter 6

Connect the world

Project: Design a webpage on a topic of your choice

In this chapter, you will:

- identify wired and wireless connections
- explain what a computer network is
- practise staying safe on the World Wide Web
- design your own webpage.

End of chapter project:

Design a webpage on a topic of your choice

You will choose a topic and design something like these webpages:

What do you already know?

- A computer system is a computer with its connected parts (components).
- Some of these components are inputs.
- Some of these components are outputs.

How do computers communicate?

Role play

Your teacher will give you cups connected with a string. Pull the string tight and talk to your partner.

Key terms

- **wired connection** – when devices communicate with each other through a wire
- **wireless connection** – when devices communicate with each other without a wire connecting the devices

Wired connections

Some computers and components communicate through wires. They use a **wired connection**.

Wire

> **Discuss:** 1. How was talking with the cups and string like a wired connection?

Workbook Page 51: Complete Task A, '**Connect the computer systems**'.

Wireless connections

When you talk to a friend this is wireless communication.

Some computers and components communicate without wires. They use a **wireless connection**.

> **Discuss:** 2. Where have you used a wireless connection?

Workbook Page 52: Complete Task B, '**Find the wireless connections**'.

Wired connections are often faster but wireless connections can be very useful.

> **Discuss:** 3. How has using a wireless connection been useful to you?

> **What do you already know?**
>
> • Some computers and components communicate through wires.
> • Some computers and components can communicate without wires.

What is a computer network?

A **computer network** is a group of computers that are connected so they can communicate.

For example, computers on the same computer network can share a printer.

Key terms

• **computer network** – group of computers connected so that they can communicate
• **internet** – big network that connects computers and digital devices around the world

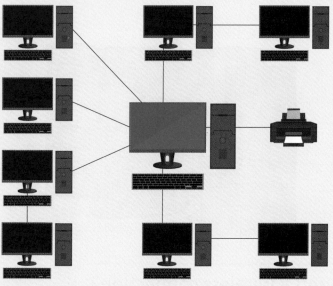

Workbook Page 53: Complete Task A, **'Connect to the printer'**.

Sending messages

Computers on the same computer network can send messages to each other.

Role play

Your teacher will now give some string to make a network. You will pass a message along the string to someone connected to you.

Discuss: 4. What happened when you had to pass the message to someone not connected to the network? What happens when a computer is not connected to a network?

Workbook Page 54: Complete Task B, '**Send a message**'.

The internet

The **internet** is a big network that connects computers and digital devices around the world.

Computers can connect to the internet with a wired or wireless connection.

Workbook Page 54: Complete Task C, '**Connecting to the internet**'.

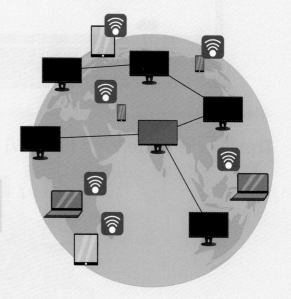

We use the internet for lots of things but there are times when the internet is not available.

Discuss: 5. Can you think of a time when you could not connect to the internet?

> **What do you already know?**
>
> - The internet is a big network that connects computers and digital devices around the world.

What is a webpage?

A **webpage** is a document that your computer gets from the internet.
A **website** is a collection of webpages.

Key terms

- **webpage** – document that your computer gets from the internet
- **website** – collection of webpages
- **World Wide Web (WWW)** – all the webpages on the internet

The **World Wide Web (WWW)** is all the webpages on the internet.

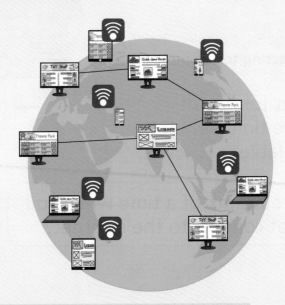

Workbook Page 55: Complete Task A, '**Fill in the letters**'.

Staying safe

Websites can be helpful and fun. Many websites are not for children, so you need to know how to stay safe.

Stay safe: Rules for staying safe:

1. Ask a grown up if you want to use a computer.
2. Tell a grown up if you see something on the computer that worries you.

Role play

In pairs, act out what you should do if you see something that worries you on a computer.

Your teacher will tell you how to visit a webpage.

Workbook Page 55: Complete Task B, '**Staying safe**'.

Discuss: 6. How can you stay safe when visiting a webpage?

What do you already know?

- A webpage is a document that your computer gets from the internet.
- There are lots of different types of website and some are not for children.

End of chapter project:

Design a webpage on a topic of your choice.

Discuss: 7. What webpages do you enjoy?

Different types of webpage

There are lots of different types of webpage, including: information, games, tutorials and online shopping.

Information

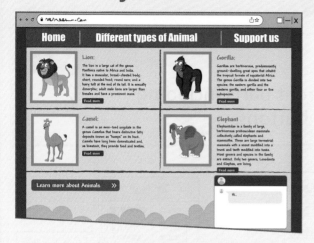

Tutorial

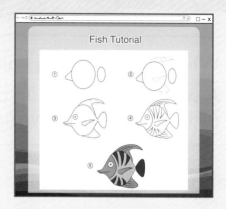

Game

Online shopping

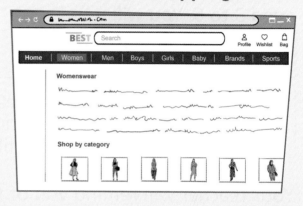

Your webpage should be about a topic that is interesting for children of your age.

Workbook Page 56: Complete Task A, '**Choose a topic**'.

Parts of a webpage

A webpage can have many different parts including: pictures, headings, writing and buttons to click on.

Workbook Page 56: Complete Task B, '**What is on a webpage?**'.

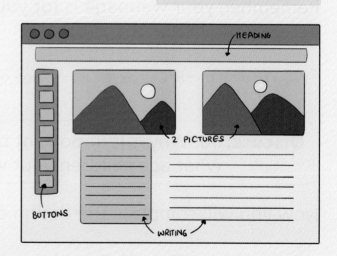

Plan your webpage

Workbook Page 57: Complete Task C, '**Plan your webpage**'.

Discuss: 8. What website ideas did you think of?

What do you already know?

- A webpage is made up of different parts including: pictures, headings, writing and buttons.

Webpage design

You are designing a webpage for young children aged 3 to 6. You will now finish your webpage design.

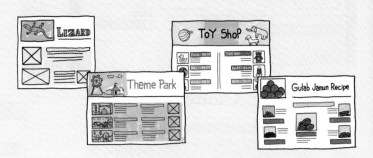

Discuss: 9. Do you like webpages with pictures? Do you like to see big headings on webpages? What other things do you like to see on webpages?

Your teacher will remind you of the comments on your webpage plans.

Design your webpage

Remember, your webpage is for young children. Make sure you design your webpage for them.

Workbook Page 58: Complete Task A, '**Age of webpage visitors**'.

Discuss: 10. Why is it important to think about what age children your website is for?

Now you will complete the design of your webpage.

Workbook Pages 58 and 59: Complete Task B, '**Design your webpage**'.

Discuss: 11. Did you change your design from your plan? Why or why not?

> **What do you already know?**
> • Showcasing means presenting a project to an audience.

Showcase your project

Remember, showcasing is a way of sharing your project with other people.

Showcase: Tips for showcasing your project:
• Hold your workbook up to show your design.
• Point at each part of your webpage when you talk about it.
• Do your best to talk clearly and loudly enough for everyone to hear.

Showcase: Showcase your webpage design. You should:
• talk about your webpage topic
• point at the parts of your webpage: header, images, writing
• say why your webpage is suitable for young children.

Workbook Page 61, Complete Task A, '**Reflection**'.

Congratulations!

Well done! You have completed Chapter 6, 'Connect the world'.

In this chapter you:

- ☑ identified wired and wireless connections

- ☑ explained what a computer network is

- ☑ practised staying safe on the World Wide Web

- ☑ designed your own webpage.

Key terms

- **computer network** – group of computers connected so that they can communicate
- **internet** – big network that connects computers and digital devices around the world

- **webpage** – document that your computer gets from the internet
- **website** – collection of webpages
- **wired connection** – when devices communicate with each other through a wire

- **wireless connection** – when devices communicate with each other without a wire connecting the devices
- **World Wide Web (WWW)** – all the webpages on the internet

Reflect: What new things did you learn about the internet and webpages?

Chapter 7
The power of data

Project: Plan a dream class celebration

In this chapter, you will:

- use a search engine and online form
- sort and organise data
- write questions to help plan a class celebration
- find the most popular class answers.

End of chapter project:

Plan a dream class celebration

You will plan something like one of these celebrations!

What do you already know?

- People ask a question to find an answer.
- The internet is a big network that connects computers and digital devices around the world.

Search for answers

People ask questions to find out information.

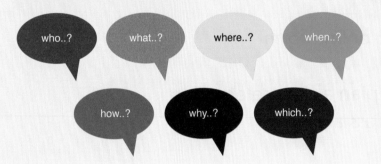

who..? what..? where..? when..?

how..? why..? which..?

Key terms

- **search engine** – app that can be used to find information from the internet
- **form** – document that helps you collect answers to more than one question

Arifah types a question into the search box.

Discuss: 1. If you have a question, where could you go to find the answer?

A **search engine** is an app that can be used to find information from the internet.

Your teacher will show you how to use a search engine.

The search engine searches the internet to find information.

Discuss: 2. Why would a search engine be a good way to find answers?

Workbook Page 62: Complete Task A, '**Search safely**'.

Stay safe: Some search engines have 'Safe Search' settings that you can use to block harmful results.

The search engine shows the answers it has found.

Ask someone a question

When you ask one person a question you find out what that person knows or what they think.

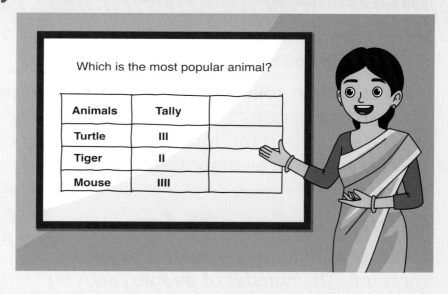

You can ask a question to more than one person. You can use a tally chart to collect answers from more than one person.

Your teacher will ask you a question, then mark your answer.

Ask someone more than one question

You can use a **form** to collect answers to more than one question.

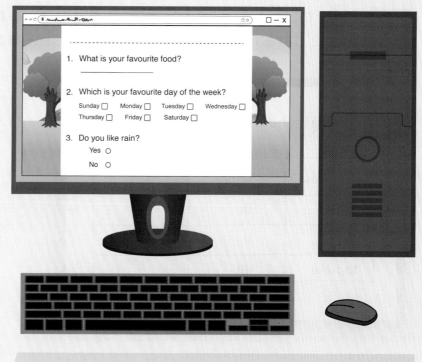

Workbook Page 63: Complete Task B, '**Fill in the form**'.

Discuss: 3. Have you filled in a form in school? What questions did you answer?

Workbook Page 63: Complete Task C, '**Reflect**'.

What do you already know?

- A tally chart collects answers to questions from more than one person.
- Order is important, for example the order of instructions in an algorithm.

Answer questions with data

Data is information you can use to answer questions. The number of people choosing each option for a meal is data. The distance each person in a class can jump is data.

Key terms

- **data** – information used to answer questions

A tally chart can be used to collect data from more than one person. The data is used to answer the question.

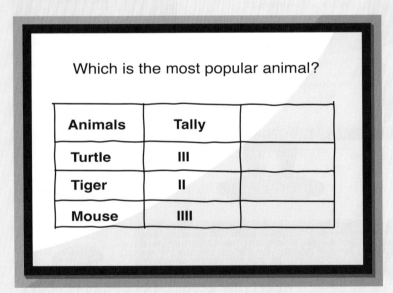

Which is the most popular animal?

Animals	Tally	
Turtle	III	
Tiger	II	
Mouse	IIII	

Discuss: 4. Which is the most popular animal? How do you know?

Sorting data

To sort data means to put it in a way that makes it easier to answer questions.

Workbook Page 64: Complete Task A, '**Count the tigers**'.

Discuss: 5. Why was it easier to count the tigers in the second picture?

Sorting and ordering data

In Chapter 3 you put your Bee-Bot instructions in order.

Sorted data can be put into an order. This makes it easier to answer questions.

Workbook Page 65: Complete Task B, '**Count the insects**'.

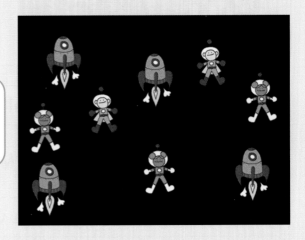

Discuss: 6. Which question in the Workbook was easiest to answer? Why?

Your teacher will give you a Scratch project to sort and order.

What do you already know?

- Data is information you use to answer questions.
- You can collect data using a form.

End of chapter project:

Plan a dream class celebration.

Discuss: 7. How do you usually celebrate things?

Workbook Page 66: Complete Task A, '**My class celebration**'.

Discuss: 8. What did you draw for your celebration?

Design a form

To plan a class celebration it is important to get data from everyone in the class.

Which food would you like to eat?	
	II
	IIII
	III

You will ask more than one question.

Discuss: 9. Do you remember what you should use to ask more than one question?

Workbook Page 67: Complete Task B, '**Our class form**'.

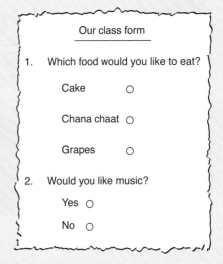

Our class form

1. Which food would you like to eat?

   Cake ○

   Chana chaat ○

   Grapes ○

2. Would you like music?

   Yes ○

   No ○

What do you already know?

- You can use a form to collect data from many people.
- Predict means use information you have now to say what is going to happen in the future.

The most popular answers from the class will help plan the celebration.

Online forms

An **online form** is a webpage with questions and spaces for answers.

When people answer questions in an online form the form collects their answers.

Key terms

- **online form** – webpage with questions for people to answer

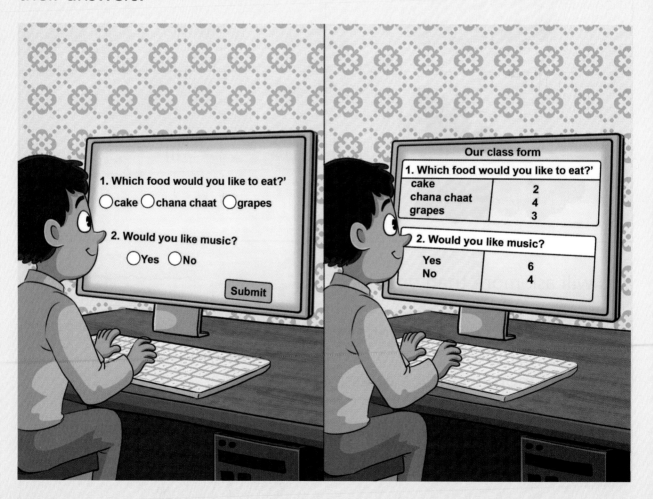

Your teacher will show you your class celebration online form.

Answer the questions

Now it is your turn. Answer the class celebration questions using the online form.

Workbook Page 68: Complete Task A, 'Online form checklist'.

Predict the answers

In Chapter 3 you used information to predict how a Bee-bot would move.

Discuss: 10. What do you know now to help you predict the most popular class answers?

Workbook Page 68: Complete Task B, 'My prediction'.

Discuss: 11. What do you predict will be the most popular class answers?

> **What do you already know?**
> • You can put data into tables to make it easier to read.

Looking at data

You can put data into tables to make it easier to read.

> **Discuss:** 12. Where have you used a data table before?

Favourite hobbies

Hobby	Number of people
reading	II
sports	III
art	IIII

Favourite fruit

Fruit	Number of people
melon	
grapes	
apple	

Favourite colours

Colour	Number of people
red	3
blue	5
pink	4

Workbook Pages 69 and 70: Complete Task A, '**Sort the tables**'.

Your teacher will share your class celebration data with you.

Workbook Page 70: Complete Task B, '**Popular choices**'.

> **Discuss:** 13. What are the most popular choices?

> **Discuss:** 14. Were your predictions correct?

> **What do you already know?**
> - The most popular answers from the class.
> - Showcasing means sharing your project with other people.

Our celebration

Pictures can be used to show data. These examples show celebrations based on the data collected by different classes.

Workbook Page 71: Complete Task A, '**Our class celebration**'.

Showcase your project

Remember, showcasing means sharing your project with other people.

Tips for showcasing your pictures:

- Hold your workbook up to show your pictures.
- Point at parts of your pictures when you talk about them.
- Do your best to talk clearly and loudly enough for everyone to hear.

Showcase: Showcase your 'My class celebration' and 'Our class celebration' pictures to someone else. You should tell them about the differences between your 'My class celebration' and your 'Our class celebration' pictures.

Workbook Page 72: Complete Task B, '**Reflection**'.

Congratulations!

Well done! You have completed Chapter 7, 'The power of data'.
In this chapter you:

- ☑ used a search engine and an online form

- ☑ sorted and organised data

- ☑ wrote questions to help plan a class celebration

- ☑ found the most popular class answers.

Key terms

- **data** – information used to answer questions

- **form** – document that helps you collect answers to more than one question

- **online form** – webpage with questions for people to answer

- **search engine** – app that can be used to find information from the internet

Reflect: How did data help you to plan your celebration?

Glossary of key terms

algorithm – set of instructions to complete a task or solve a problem

app (program) – used for specific tasks on a computer

Bee-Bot – robot that uses code to move in different directions

capital letters – big letters that we use at the start of a sentence or a name; capital letters are bigger than lowercase letters

code – instructions that tell a computer what to do

code block – single line of code in Scratch

component – part of a computer system

computer – electronic machine that can perform tasks

computer network – group of computers connected so that they can communicate

computer system – computer with its connected parts

costume – different options for how your sprite looks in Scratch; it is like the clothes you wear each day

data – information used to answer questions

debugging – finding errors in code and fixing them

digital device – object that contains a small computer to perform tasks

form – document that helps you collect answers to more than one question

headphones – component that can play sound from a computer

input – component that allows a person to enter information into a computer

internet – big network that connects computers and digital devices around the world

interview – a discussion with a person, where you ask questions to find things out

keyboard – component that you use to type letters and numbers on a computer

layers – placing objects on top of each other, for example a cake could have three layers of sponge

log off – exiting a computer when you have finished using it

log on – entering a username and password to use a computer

lowercase letters – smaller letters that we use most of the time when we write and type; lowercase letters are smaller than capital letters

microphone – component that can get sound into a computer

mouse – component that you move to point to things on a computer screen

online form – webpage with questions for people to answer

open – view a file on a computer

output – component that presents information to a person

password – secret code you use to keep your information safe

predict – use information you have now to say what is going to happen in the future

printer – component that can put pictures and words on paper

robot – digital device that performs a useful task on its own; a robot may be able to move or talk

save – save a file on a computer so that you can use it again next time

Scratch – program that allows you to create your own programs or apps

screen (or monitor) – component that shows pictures and videos from a computer

search engine – app that can be used to find information from the internet

showcase – present a project to an audience

speakers – component that can play sound from a computer

sprite – character or object in Scratch

stage – area in Scratch where you can play with your app

touchpad (or trackpad) – part of a laptop computer that you use to point to things on a computer screen by moving your finger

touchscreen – component that shows pictures and videos and allows you to point to things with your finger

username – personal name you use to access your information, for example to use a computer at school

webcam – component that can get pictures and video into a computer

webpage – document that your computer gets from the internet

website – collection of webpages

wired connection – when devices communicate with each other through a wire

wireless connection – when devices communicate with each other without a wire connecting the devices

word processor – a program you use to type words into a computer to create a document

World Wide Web (WWW) – all the webpages on the internet

Acknowledgements

Screenshots

Support materials and screenshots are licensed under the Creative Commons Attribution-ShareAlike 2.0 license. We are grateful to the following for permission to reproduce screenshots. In some instances, we have been unable to trace the owners of copyright material, and we would appreciate any information that would enable us to do so.

Scratch Foundation: Authorised usage of screenshots showcasing Scratch programming environment elements.

Scratch is developed by the Lifelong Kindergarten Group at the MIT Media Lab: p.21-23, p.43-49, p.53, p.55, p.58-60, p.79.

Images

We are grateful for the following for permission to reproduce their images:

p.2 Den Rozhnovsky/Shutterstock, p.2 Lukas Gojda/Shutterstock, p.2 Issarawat Tattong/Shutterstock, p.2 Miguel Lagoa/ Shutterstock, p.2 SlayStorm/Shutterstock, p.2 vovan/Shutterstock, p.3 JOCA_PH/Shutterstock, p.3 Stefan.Simonovski/ Shutterstock, p.3 monticello/Shutterstock, p.3 Prostock-studio/Shutterstock, p.4 Naypong Studio/Shutterstock, p.4 pixinoo/ Shutterstock, p.4 phototiara/Shutterstock, p.4 KerrysWorld/Shutterstock, p.4 Dean Drobot/Shutterstock, p.5 Juan Enrique del Barrio/Shutterstock, p.5 Suwin66/Shutterstock, p.5 Abaca Press/Alamy Stock Photo, p.40 indigolotos/Shutterstock, p.40 Anton Starikov/Shutterstock, p.40 NooMUboN Photo/Shutterstock, p.40 Eakkapon Sriharun/Shutterstock, p.40 Kitch Bain/Shutterstock, p.40 Voronin76/Shutterstock, p.40 Kamil Zajaczkowski/Shutterstock, p.40 szefei/Shutterstock, p.41 IVAN ROSHCHUPKIN/Shutterstock, p.41 Studio_Fennel/Shutterstock, p.41 Dzmitry Kliapitski / Alamy Stock Photo.